Root Cellar Construction Handbook

Your Root Cellaring Guide for Learning How to Build a Natural Cold Storage for Preserving Vegetables, Fruits, and Other Foods

By

Fiona Begum

Disclaimer

This publication is designed to provide competent and reliable information regarding the subject matter covered. However, the views expressed in this publication are those of the author alone, and should not be taken as expert instruction or professional advice. The reader is responsible for his or her own actions.

The author hereby disclaims any responsibility or liability whatsoever that is incurred from the use or application of the contents of this publication by the

1

purchaser or reader. The purchaser or reader is hereby responsible for his or her own actions.

Table of Contents

Introduction

Suppose you depend on fresh produce grown nearby, in your personal nursery, or purchased at the neighborhood farmers' market; in that case, you are likely aware of the challenge of storing seasonal produce without freezing it. Root cellars have been a means of preserving vegetables for those who want to retain their most normal state; fresh and appealing.

To call root cellaring revolutionary may seem over the top, but the changes it might make to your food can be life-altering. This simple, age-old concept of burying your food can form the cornerstone of a more holistic diet and lifestyle while also making healthy eating more practical and significantly more economical.

Before deciding whether a root cellar is something you want to own, let's first understand what it is and how it functions. A root cellar is a compartment dug into the ground where you can store food to protect and preserve its freshness while also slowing its decay rate. Since the climate is optimal for food preservation, you can store everything from root vegetables to rhubarb wine underground.

For millennia, storing foods in a root cellar during the cold weather months when nothing grew was the only way most people could endure. All of that has changed thanks to modern refrigeration, and most of us have had no trouble since the end of World War II finding, for example, berries at the local supermarket in the middle of February.

Today's food is often the outcome of a procedure our great-grandmothers would not have recognized. Seasonal produce was consumed by our great-grandmothers, and rather than storing food in the freezer, they kept it underground. We must grow and store food if we wish to consume the produce the earlier generations would have considered proper food.

Having a root cellar or other cold storage rooms is highly recommended assuming that you plan to grow part of what you eat or you choose to purchase products in bulk for processing. The root cellar provides a convenient location to protect your produce over the winter, enabling you to serve fresh, wholesome foods while saving money on your grocery expenses. Basic underground root cellars are easy to build, and the soil's natural insulation helps to keep food fresh for many months by maintaining the right temperature and humidity.

This book is packed with valuable tips and pointers to enable you to begin your root cellaring journey on the right foot. So, buckle up and join me in the next chapter as we get things off the ground.

Chapter 1

Fundamentals of Root Cellars

What is a Root Cellar?

Root cellars are storage spaces usually built underground or partly underground. Root cellars leverage the earth's cooling and insulating properties and consistent humidity levels to produce a stable storage environment. It is a time-tested preservation technique, whether you fill up a root cellar with produce grown yourself or from the local growers' marketplace.

A root cellar is often used to preserve root crops such as parsnips, carrots, beets, rutabagas, potatoes, and turnips. The environment is also suitable for storing perennial flowers' bulbs or rhizomes as well as jars of pickled or canned vegetables. A root cellar can also be used as a storage area for wine, beer, or other homebrewed alcoholic beverages.

Nowadays, with nearly every home having a refrigerator, sustainability and minimizing food waste are frequently the primary motivations for root cellaring. Beyond that, keeping a root cellar is quite inexpensive as far as both money and energy consumption is concerned.

Pros and Cons of Root Cellars

Owing a root cellar comes with some benefits and disadvantages. Let's take a look at them.

Pros

1. Greater food security - A root cellar allows you to keep many months' worth of food in storage at once. It enables you to become more independent.

   You can stay in your home for many weeks, even during an emergency where a road or bridge floods out, without being able to go to the market or during a winter snowstorm.

2. Keeps food in storage longer - Your freezer or refrigerator can only hold so much food at once.

If you want to store a large number of potatoes and squash, a root cellar is a necessity.

3. Reduces costs - A root cellar can still help you cut costs, saving you money even if you can't grow all the food you or your family consumes. In harvest season, you can purchase vegetables and fruits in large quantities. Produce is most affordable and fresh during that time. Then you may store it and preserve it all year long for consumption in your root cellar.

4. Reduced dependence on electricity - Root cellars continue to function even when there is a power outage since they don't rely on electricity to store food.

Cons

1. Costly to construct - A root cellar is a modest outbuilding on your land, similar to a shed. The materials required for construction will cost several thousand dollars. The price of renting any equipment you don't already own must also be taken into account.

2. Requires lots of work to construct - The construction of a root cellar necessitates a great deal of manual effort, including moving around cinder blocks, concrete, and dirt.

   If you work a full-time job, you likely only have a couple of hours each day to devote to your root cellar. In that situation, finishing the entire project can require several weeks.

3. There is a learning curve - Each root cellar is unique. The conditions are not as consistent as in a refrigerator since you're depending on the earth to preserve your produce. The coolest and warmest parts of your root cellar need to be identified. Additionally, you will need to be cognizant of what items you are preserving and the environmental conditions it prefers.

4. Maintenance - You must maintain a high degree of humidity and keep the floor moistened. You might need to cover some veggies with damp cloths because some vegetables prefer to be damper than others. You must also clean your

root cellar if mold or mildew starts to grow before it gets out of control.

5. Inconvenient - If the root cellar is not next to your house, going there to gather food can be a hassle. Particularly during the bitter winter months or when it is raining heavily.

Types of Root Cellars

Root cellars are essentially just underground caves. There are various ways to build this cave, each with its own advantages and disadvantages. Let's take a look at some of the well know root cellars.

Underground

Historically, root cellars were constructed underground. The top of the roof was occasionally left uncovered for ventilation (an A-frame root cellar). The root cellar could also be completely buried beneath the ground.

Underground, the humidity and temperature conditions are both constant. The root cellar's surrounding earth serves as a natural insulator and provides the appropriate conditions for preserving produce.

You must be aware of your region's frost line before excavating an underground root cellar. For instance, the frost line is about 18" into the earth in the Northeastern United States. To prevent produce from freezing and to keep it cool, you must store it below this line (the roof could be above the frost line but will have to be insulated). To reach a cold, stable temperature, anticipate having to dig at least 4 to 6 ft into the ground.

You should know about the water table too. Assuming the water table is excessively high around the area, excavating the ground wouldn't be an option since it would bring about flooding of the root cellar.

Pros

1. Adequately maintains a stable humidity and temperature

Cons

1. Vertical doors can be tough to get in snowy weather

2. Accessible via a ladder or steep stairs

3. Renting of backhoe excavator can be costly

4. Might demand drainage to prevent erosion

In a Hill

If your home or land has a hill, then a root cellar can be dug directly into the hill. Usually, the construction process is a little bit easy; however, the roof and walls would have to be braced. Per the hill's size, you may need to recess the root cellar into the ground so that food storage is achieved below the frost line.

The nice thing about an in-hill root cellar is likely the ease of access: the root cellar can be easily accessed without needing to climb down a ladder. A horizontal door requires no shoveling to remove snow from it.

With in-hill root cellars, drainage problems are typically nonexistent. It's feasible to tilt the root cellar's floor, so any water that penetrates just flows out the door

The drawback is that not every land or home comes with a hill. Even then, the hill may not be located in a place that is accessible. Are you up for going out every day in the winter through the snow to your property's edge to get vegetables?

Pros

1. Elevated entrance

2. Absence of steep stairs or ladders

3. Drainage is typically not an issue.

4. Less prone to flooding

Cons

1. Needs a hill on the property

2. May possibly not be close to home

3. Bracing the roof against a hill's weight is necessary

Above Ground

You can still construct a root cellar that's above-ground even if your land or home doesn't have a hill. Typically, this entails building a concrete structure and surrounding it with earth. You could also build with "earth bags" rather than concrete blocks.

Drainage is the biggest problem with root cellars that are above-ground. Your strategy to avoid this will need you to employ floor drains or find a technique to redirect water away from the root cellar.

An above-ground root cellar may not maintain a sufficiently cold temperature. In essence, these become "cold rooms" as opposed to actual root cellars.

Pros

1. Can be constructed close to the kitchen

2. Usually quick and affordable to construct

3. An entrance that is above ground

4. Absence of steep stairs or ladders

Cons

1. Drainage is a frequent issue.

2. Maintaining a cold temperature is challenging

Attached to a Home

Under some circumstances, you might be able to convert a portion of your home into a root cellar, such as;

- The area underneath your deck or porch

- A section of your basement

- A section of your garage

- A room you excavated beside your basement, with a door from the basement leading there.

The consequence of the above makes the root cellar conveniently accessible. There wouldn't be a need for you to walk through the snow to collect your vegetables. Additionally, you won't need to clear snow away from the front of the entrance door.

However, you should exercise caution while converting a portion of your house or anything connected to it into a root cellar. Because of the difference in temperature between your home and the root cellar, moisture and mold issues may arise. Additionally, you'll need to ventilate the root cellar with extreme caution.

Pros

1. A location that is easily accessible

2. Convenient

3. Can be constructed quickly and easily

Cons

1. It might lead to mold problems

2. Requires close attention to insulation and ventilation

Cost to Build a Root Cellar

You'll need a way to excavate a hole that's the size of a room, and renting a backhoe is the most realistic option to get this done. Whether it be masonry, concrete, or wood, you'll also need supplies to construct your cellar. Make certain it can withstand the soil's weight.

It's possible that you'll require a skilled builder to create the roof's shape. You don't want to experience a cave-in that might ruin your harvest or possibly do someone harm. A flat roof is also inappropriate since it would cause moisture to accumulate all around, which will lead to mildew and mold problems.

The cost varies according to factors like size, design, construction materials, etc. It might just cost a few hundred dollars to build a modest, simpler root cellar. A bigger root cellar will typically set you back thousands of dollars (around $2500 to $25000). Materials are the largest expense when constructing a root cellar. The cost might be significantly reduced if you can repurpose the materials. Remember that a root cellar saves you money and raises the value of your home. A root cellar can also serve as a shelter from storms. If you construct your root cellar to serve two purposes, you can qualify for financial aid from the Federal Emergency Management Agency (FEMA). This is true for both new construction and retrofits.

Chapter 2

Storing Food In a Root Cellar

What Food Can Be Stored?

When your root cellar is constructed, what produce can be stored in it, you may ask. You might have envisioned that 19th-century root cellars were stocked with bags of potatoes and bushels of apples. Root cellars today aren't all that different. Let's take a look at the kinds of things you can store in your root cellar.

Ethylene Producers

There should be many shelves in a root cellar, some of which must be above others and nearer to the vents than others. Keeping hazardous gases far from other produce kept on the lower shelves or the ground involves positioning ethylene producers (as seen below) higher up and closer to the outtake vents.

The following fruits and vegetables release ethylene gas:

- Apples.
- Apricots.
- Avocados.
- Bananas.
- Blueberries.
- Cabbage.
- Cantaloupe.
- Chinese cabbage.
- Citrus fruits (except grapefruit).
- Cranberries.
- Figs.
- Guavas.
- Grapes.
- Green onions.
- Honeydew.
- Kiwi.
- Mangoes.
- Melons.
- Mushrooms.
- Nectarines.
- Okra.
- Papaya.
- Passion fruits.
- Peaches.
- Pears.

- Peppers.
- Persimmons.
- Pineapples.
- Plantains.
- Plums.
- Prunes.
- Quinces.
- Tomatoes.
- Watermelon.

Ethylene gas can cause damage to the following fruits and vegetables:

- Asparagus.
- Broccoli.
- Brussels sprouts.
- Cabbages.
- Carrots.
- Cauli Flowers.
- Eggplants.
- Endive.
- Escarole.
- Green beans.
- Kale.
- Leafy greens.

- Lettuce.
- Parsley.
- Peas.
- Potatoes.
- Spinach.
- Squash.
- Sweet potatoes.
- Watercress.
- Yams.

Root Crops

Root crops such as winter radishes, celeriac, parsnips, beets, and horseradish should be stored in boxes filled with sawdust or loose soil to protect them from gaseous emissions. Choose a high, secluded location for odorous foods like cabbages and onions since they give off smells that impair other fruits and vegetables' flavors.

Other Foods

Root cellars are ideal places to store beer, cider, wine, and fresh produce. Low temperatures (below 40°F) are ideal for preserving cured foods like bacon, smoked meats, ham, and dairy products like cheese, cream, and milk.

In root cellars, grains and nuts can be preserved quite well, but boxes or jars must be tightly closed to avoid an insect invasion. Dried or canned foods can also be preserved, but they must be stored in a less damp cellar or in a different, drier section of the same root cellar.

Root Cellaring Success Tips

Below are some essential tips to be kept at the back of your mind while preparing to preserve your foods in a root cellar.

1. Root cellar food storage is frequently plagued by rodent issues. Placing metal wire netting at access points, like vents, is a smart idea. Ensure that the lids on all containers and jars are tightly sealed. Pest issues can be greatly reduced by keeping the space clean. Try hanging your produce if rodents are a concern rather than placing the produce on the ground.

2. Insect infestations could be a concern if you keep grains or nuts in the cellar. AVOID using an

insecticide (for a variety of reasons)! It might damage a large portion of your food storage. Bay leaves and other potent herbs can safely repel insects.

3. Only preserve perfect food in your root cellar. Use damaged vegetables and fruits for other purposes, such as canning or dehydrating.

4. Start with the smallest produce and any produce that has been somewhat marked before moving on to the largest as your supplies are used up

5. Before you harvest, a little touch of frost on cabbage, horseradish, brussels sprouts, pumpkins, turnips, rutabagas, and beets taste better and preserve well enough

6. The air can occasionally condense in root cellars that have high humidity, which is an issue. Vegetables and fruits will spoil if condensation falls from the ceiling and touches them. To prevent the spread of infections from the dripping water, a disinfectant such as chlorine should be used in pretreating the ceiling

7. You might want another door to help shelter the cellar in extremely cold conditions.

Preparing and Storing Foods in a Root Cellar

Vegetables and fruits can be stored in a root cellar in a number of ways.

1. Choose Late-Maturing Crops

Crops are more inclined to remain fresh throughout the winter if they're harvested later in the season. Avoid delaying your harvest so late to the point where you have to bother about frost. But sowing and harvesting with preservation at heart will keep your vegetables from lying in your root cellar more than is required

2. Choose Preservation Crops

Each vegetable has a variety that has been cultivated specifically for preservation. Therefore, pay attention to any kinds that are ideal for preservation when purchasing seeds or seedlings.

3. Avoid Washing Your Produce

Rather than washing your veggies and fruits before storing them in the root cellar, just clean them using a dry cloth. Your veggies will soak up more water after being washed, making them more likely to rot. If you really must wash your vegetables because they are particularly dirty, make sure their surface is dried with a dry cloth before you store them. That will assist in taking some of the extra moisture away.

4. Cure Vegetables Before Storing (If necessary)

Before storing some veggies, they must undergo curing. Your vegetables' skins get thicker after curing, extending their storage life.

Before being put in storage, potatoes, squash, garlic, and onions must all be cured. The method for curing them will vary from crop to crop.

Squash and onions can be cured by merely leaving them outside in the sun for some days. For a week or two, you may also spread them out on a wire rack. Potatoes should be kept in a dark, humid, moderate temperature, well-ventilated location for around a week to cure.

5. Inspect Your Produce Before Storage

Rot is another frequent issue. Do you recall the proverb, "One bad apple spoils the whole bunch"? Yes, that is true! Crops that have been damaged are not just likely to rot faster. Additionally, they can contaminate your healthy crops with mold and other toxins. Frequently inspect your produce and discard any rotten vegetables or other food immediately before you store them.

6. Keep Food From Freezing in Your Root Cellar

Your root cellar's main objective is to keep your produce cool but not frozen. Freezing will change the quality of your veggies, making them soggy. Your produce is also more likely to decay when it is frozen and unfrozen.

7. Be Familiar with Your Root Cellar

Various parts will be cooler or warmer than some others, even within a modest root cellar. Carrots and beets will thrive when you store them low in your root cellar, which is the coolest place to store them. Crops like tomatoes or squash love to be a little warmer, so it is best to have them stored high up the shelves.

8. Observe Conditions Using Tools

Your vegetables and fruit will have a shorter time in storage if the root cellar is opened too frequently due to changes in temperature and humidity. Typically you want to install humidity and temperature sensors outside of your root cellar. In this manner, you can check the cellars' condition without going into the cellar.

9. Keep Crops That Produce Ethylene Apart from Others

Some plants emit a gas called ethylene that speeds up the ripening process.

Apples, bananas, melons, peaches, and pears yield a lot of ethylene when harvested. Tomatoes also produce a fair amount. Do not mix these fruits with other veggies. To keep the gas contained, you might want to wrap them.

Numerous vegetables, including carrots, cabbage, green beans, and broccoli, are susceptible to ethylene, and you should store them very far; otherwise, they will get too ripe and begin to get rotten quickly.

Refer to the beginning of this chapter for ethylene-producing crops and crops it can damage.

10. Preserve Crops With Strong Smells Away From Others

Some foods, like turnips and cabbage, have a pungent smell. If they are stored among other vegetables and fruits, they can absorb the odor.

11. Your Root Cellar Should Be Kept Moist, But Not Wet or Damp

Vegetables that begin to shrink indicate that the humidity level in your root cellar has become too low. To help retain moisture within, you can cover your vegetables with straw, moist (but not wet) leaves, or other materials.

A gallon of water can also be added to the root cellar to increase the humidity

Things to Note

1. Onions and garlic should be kept on shelves that are higher, dryer, and warmer. Storage in trays enables suitable ventilation. Additionally, if the onion starts to rot, it may be detected and removed immediately before ruining the entire batch.

2. Potatoes should be placed near the floor, which is cooler and more humid (but not wet, since excess moisture will lead to rot). Wrap them with a sack to keep the light away while yet allowing air and preventing green potatoes.

3. Some cabbages should be put on the upper shelf. Squash and pumpkins should be stored on the upper shelf of the root cellar or the floor of the preserving cabinet. They prefer it to be a bit dryer and warmer.

4. Vegetables should be kept in boxes, buckets, or bins filled with sawdust, lightly wet leaves, or sand. Choose the one that works well for you.

5. When fresh produce is kept in a root cellar, it lasts for varying amounts of time, with potatoes and

apples lasting the longest. Turnips, cabbage, kohlrabi, onions, beets, garlic, winter squash, and pumpkins are other good keepers.

6. Likewise, dried peppers, beans, and nuts have exceptionally long shelf lives.

Storage Conditions for Common Foods

The recommended root cellar storage conditions are shown in the following table. You'll notice that a lot of fruits and vegetables need an environment with a high temperature and low humidity. Most individuals build a multi-room root cellar as a solution to this issue. Then you could maintain each room at the appropriate temperature for a particular crop.

Food	Temp (F)	Humidity	Shelf Life
Apples	32-40	80-90%	2-7 months
Beans, dry	32-50	65-70%	1 year
Beets	32	95%	1-3 months
Brussels Sprouts	32	90-95%	3-5 weeks
Cabbage	32	90-95%	3-4 months
Carrots	32	90-95%	4-6 months
Cauliflower	32	90-95%	2-4 weeks
Celeriac	32	90-95%	3-4 months
Celery	32	90-95%	2-3 months
Garlic	32	65-70%	6-7 months

Horseradish	30-32	90-95%	10-12 months
Kale	32	90-95%	10-14 days
Leeks	32	90-95%	1-3 months
Onions	32	65-70%	5-8 months
Parsnips	32	90-95%	2-6 months
Pears	32-40	80-90%	2-3 months
Peppers, dry	32-50	60-70%	6 months
Potatoes	38-40	90%	5-8 months
Pumpkins	50-55	70-75%	2-3 months
Salsify	32	90-95%	2-4 months
Sweet Potato	55-60	85-90%	4-6 months
Tomatoes, green	55-60	85-90%	2-6 weeks
Turnips	32	90-95%	4-5 months
Winter Radishes	32	90-95%	2-4 months
Winter Squash	50-55	70-75%	3-6 months

Another way to think about root cellar storage conditions is to group produce that requires a similar range of humidity and temperature:

Very Cold, Very Moist (32-40F/90-95% Humidity)	Cold and Moist 32-40F/80-90% Humidity	Cool and Dry (32-50F/60-70% Humidity)	Warmer and Humid (50-60F/85-90% Humidity)	Warmer and Dry (50-60F/60-70% Humidity)
Beets	Potatoes	Garlic	Sweet potatoes	Winter squash
Brussels sprouts	Apples	Onions	Tomatoes, green	Pumpkin
Carrots	Pears	Dry beans		
Cauliflower	Cabbage	Dry peppers		
Celeriac				
Celery				
Horseradish				
Kale				
Leeks				
Parsnips				
Salsify				
Turnips				
Winter radishes				

Note:

There are some disparities in what is considered to be the "optimal" temperature and humidity levels for certain crops. I utilized the most frequently listed guidelines from reliable sources to create these tables.

Chapter 3

Planning and Constructing a Root Cellar

Root Cellar Construction Requirements

The following are some factors you should consider controlling when building your root cellar:

Temperature

For proper functioning, a root cellar should be kept at a temperature of 32 to 45 °F (0 to 5 °C.). Hazardous organisms can develop and multiply in a root cellar that is too warm. Vegetables and fruits can remain fresher for a longer period if your root cellar is kept cool. A proper root cellar maintains your produce at a temperature that prevents it from freezing in the winter.

You should have a thermometer in your root cellar to monitor and measure the temperature.

Humidity

Your root cellar's level of humidity should range from 85% to 95%. In the absence of this, your vegetables will begin to shrivel, losing moisture through evaporation. Ordinarily, soil contains a lot of moisture. Thus, keeping a dirt floor in your root cellar is typically sufficient to maintain a good amount of humidity. If you decide that's insufficient, you can also cover your produce with sawdust, sand, burlap sacks, straw, or other items that are damp but not wet.

Have a hydrometer placed in your root cellar to monitor the humidity level. Check on it frequently.

Ventilation

Is ventilation necessary in a root cellar? In most circumstances, yes.

Adequate ventilation is essential to prevent excess moisture and ethylene gas from accumulating in your root cellar. Your produce may suddenly turn moldy or overripe due to the absence of proper ventilation. For optimal airflow, your root cellar must have an intake for air and outflow vents. To take in cool air from the outside, inbound air vents ought to be placed close to the ground.

Because warm air rises, outflow vents in the root cellar should be higher, near the roof. For maximum results, position your root cellar's inflow and outflow on the opposing sides of the room.

Darkness

Many plants use light as a signal to begin sprouting. Your root cellar should be as dark as it can get to stop this from occurring. Ensure that your entrances are completely sealed to prevent sunlight from entering. Of course, you will need a source of light to view your produce. You can utilize a headlamp if you do not want to introduce electricity into your root cellar. Additionally, make sure to switch off any lights in your root cellar anytime you are not there. You can also consider installing a timer if you decide to introduce electricity. In this manner, if you mistakenly leave the light on, it won't damage your produce.

Accessibility

A root cellar is of no use if it's unused. Thoroughly examine w What type is most appropriate for you. Building an underground root cellar, for instance, is pointless if you have to climb a ladder or walk down steep stairs to enter inside.

Examine these things to make sure your root cellar is accessible:

- Your kitchen or garden's closeness

- How you're going to get in (steps, ladder, walk-in)

- If snow will block the door or the way to the entrance becomes slippery

- Do you utilize carts or wheelbarrows? Can they go past the door? Do you require a staircase?

- Whether a canopy over the doorway is required

Size

The amount of food an average family would require for the cold season may be stored in a relatively small space. A root cellar that is 8 by 8 feet should be sufficient. All that a family might produce can be stored if the space is expanded to 10 by 10 feet. However, in other circumstances, you might prefer a bigger root cellar. For instance, if you intend to use the root cellar both as a shelter from the storm and as a bunker.

Try to enter a building of comparable size to yours to have an idea of the size your root cellar ought to be (e.g., a shed). Be mindful of the height of the ceiling. The root cellar could result in less usage if you bend to get in.

Construct a multi-room root cellar if you intend to store produce that demands various levels of temperature and humidity. The produce that needs a greater temperature and/or less humidity should be positioned in the area that is nearest to the door.

Having an impenetrable wall and door between every room in multi-room root cellars is critical. You should also think about ventilation. Every area needs its unique ventilation system.

Materials

The choice of materials is important, especially in light of how well they'll control humidity. You should also consider materials that can allow water to exit if you think drainage may be a problem.

Here is a list of the available choice of materials you can use for the shelf, walls, roof, and floor.

1. Floor

The simplest and least expensive choice is a dirt floor, particularly one dug into the earth or a hillside. Dirt is excellent in controlling humidity. Nevertheless, dirt is a bad choice if the earth is especially moist or dry. Additionally, gravel floors are affordable and simple. To boost the humidity in dry weather, water can be sprayed over the gravel and aid with drainage when wet.

A lot of people prefer cement floors. Because cement is so effective at holding and collecting water, it increases humidity in arid environments.

Some people cover the ground of their root cellar with sand. To improve the humidity, you can spray some water on it. But in my opinion, this is a terrible plan. Regardless of how meticulous you are about taking off your shoes, sand will always find its way inside your house since it sticks to your shoes quickly.

Tip

Keep in mind that your root cellar may have two distinct floor types. For instance, one area could have a cement floor for foods that need high humidity, and the other could have a dirt floor for foods that need low humidity.

2. Walls

A root cellar's walls serve as retaining walls. As a result, even though using dirt walls is an option, your root cellar risk quickly collapsing due to the ground's weight just above.

Concrete blocks should nearly always be used for the walls since they make the most sense. These are among the least expensive choices and can be simply fortified with steel. The walls might theoretically be made of wood. But ultimately, these will deteriorate and need to be replaced. It is preferable to select a more durable material if you do not wish to bother about your walls falling inward.

Some people lay complete cargo containers in the ground to utilize them as a root cellar. The cargo container, unfortunately, will ultimately rust and probably have drainage issues. Therefore, unless you already have a spare cargo container lying around, using one is not a wise long-term decision.

3. Ceiling

In most cases, poured concrete is the wisest choice. It is sturdy enough to resist the weight of the earth above it when adequately fortified. You overlay the concrete with dirt after it has been poured in and has dried. Although you might be inclined to expose your root cellar's roof to erect an outbuilding above it or use it as a patio, this is often a bad idea.

For a root cellar to keep a constant temperature and humidity, it must be dug several feet into the ground. They would not operate properly if there is no dirt above them. Ensure the ceiling is well insulated if you intend to put a structure above it.

4. Shelves and doors

For your root cellar to be functional, it will require lots of shelves. You will also require a door that is both airtight and simple to open. The appropriate material for these two is typically wood. Wood has the drawback of rotting ultimately. Pick a wood type like black locust, teak, bald cypress, or California redwood with good rot resistance. Even though these are quite costly, they will benefit you in the long run since you won't need to change your shelves every few years. Never use treated wood of any kind.

Drainage

Drought is occurring more frequently. To prevent your produce from being flooded, you will definitely need a drainage system, even if you reside in an area with a low water table and dry soil. This can be accomplished by creating a space between the walls and the ground. These openings are filled with drainage pipes that divert water out of the root cellar. The spaces are subsequently filled with gravel to help with the flow of water.

Other options, like putting a thick coat of gravel on the ground, sloping the floor, or constructing a drainage hole, may also be effective.

Tips to Keep Your Root Cellar Cool

Take into account these hints to optimize the environment in your root cellar:

- The temperature is completely stable at a depth of around 10 feet (3 m).

- Avoid digging a root cellar close to a big tree since the roots will gradually spread and weaken the walls of the root cellar.

- Wood is not a quick carrier of cold and heat, unlike metal; thus, wooden platforms, bins, and wood shelves are typically used inside the cellar

- Position shelves 1-3" (3-8 cm) from the walls to allow for air movement, which is essential for reducing airborne mold.

- The best outdoor root cellar floor is filled dirt. For a root cellar in a basement, concrete functions effectively and is feasible.

- Root cellars must have monitoring devices for measuring humidity levels and temperatures, such as a hygrometer and thermometer. If at all practicable, these conditions should be regularly inspected.

46

- Heat is frequently controlled through ventilation to the outside or an exhaust pipe.

Building an Underground Root Cellar

Having discussed several aspects of the root cellar construction requirements, it's time to get to work demonstrating how I built my root cellar around my property.

First Step: The hole

Excavate a hole underground. Fortunately for me, I have a neighborhood gravedigger who is artistic in using a backhoe.

Remember the depth in size an underground hole should be for the temperature stability of your root cellar? For this cellar, I used the 8 by 8 feet size; you can also use the 10 by 10 feet size if you want your root cellar to be bigger.

Second Step: The footer

Concrete footer should be poured in for the walls.

Third Step: Position the blocks

Begin to lay the blocks. Around 320 blocks were used in this 8 by 8 feet root cellar.

Poured concrete for the ceiling is the exciting part that comes next. You wouldn't want a plain flat slab since you'd need the condensation from the ceiling to flow to the sides. For the ceiling, I made a plywood structure that has an arched top. A sturdier roof would as well be created by the arch. Moreover, it creates an extremely robust form.

Fourth Step: Construct the shape for the roof

I constructed the shape for the ceiling in a carpentry workshop and then took it apart. ½" plywood is used for the arches, which were then pushed into a 2x4 dado groove. Consequently, a very sturdy structure was constructed.

Fifth Step: Assemble the shape on the ceiling

I put the shape back together on the walls of the root cellar after I was happy with the shape I had constructed. Reinforced by three vertical 2x4s on every side, the fit is good and snug.

Not seen in the image are eight 1/2" pieces of plywood measuring 6 by 23 inches, which were attached after the plywood sheets had been installed. They serve as additional reinforcing pillars wedged between the plywood sheets and the 2x4s' top.

The plywood, a plastic sheet, and several ½ rebars are next in this assembly. Multiple rebars. Why not? Rebar is inexpensive. The estimated load rating would be about 250 pounds/square foot if this were to be a flat 4" slab; more than sufficient. It is up to 5" thick and arched, though. Additionally, the rebar is cemented in place, extending a foot into the walls. I'm unsure of the load rating presently, but it's far more sufficient.

Sixth Step: Rebar and pouring of concrete on the roof

Eighteen ½" rebars were placed on 8" centers. Robust enough!

Pour concrete into the ceiling shape after adding a perimeter to it; the equivalence of 4,000 pounds. Given that my five arches were supporting all of that weight, I had anticipated at least a slight distortion of my shape, but there wasn't any; awesome!

Out of caution, I waited until I was certain the concrete was completely dried before going into the cellar

Since the shape was made to be easily disassembled and reused, detaching it from the inside wasn't hard.

Below is an image of the top before the doorway was finished, with two feet of dirt covering the cellar. To shield people from harm, the rebar's ends are covered by the wood at the rear. This will be a part of the entranceway's reinforcement.

The roof was poured into three portions since that's the amount of concrete I can handle while working singlehandedly. The joints are almost undetectable from underneath, and they're waterproofed. Using regular concrete, it was simple to create the upper arch. The upper arch's radius is roughly 6 inches bigger than its lower counterpart.

Seventh Step: Finishing the inside

Owing to the plastic sheet I placed over the plywood, the ceiling is as polished as a countertop. See the image below of light bouncing off the ceiling.

A great root cellar equipped for many vegetables and fruits is made by adding stairs and doors above and below. Presently, I am happy with the results of preserving apples, carrots, potatoes, etc. At the side, one of the two 4" vents is visible. The other is on the opposite side of the cellar.

I constructed the stairway with its half on a foundation at ground level and the other half slightly beneath the frost line to save cost on materials and labor. Digging the whole stairs down to the ground level would only create a big inaccessible gap. Ensure to go through all the factors you must consider when building your root cellar, as discussed in the beginning parts of this chapter, and incorporate them in your root cellar construction.

Root Cellar Construction Alternatives

Having shed some light on the construction of an underground root cellar, as seen above, let's attempt to replicate something similar, but in this case, an alternate root cellar that's less costly to construct using some of your reusable household items.

Sunken Fridge or Freezer

Underground root cellars are, in most cases, the recommended method to store your produce using the earth's natural cold temperature; however, when resources and time are limited, you work with what you have. This leads me to how you can construct a compact yet functional sunken fridge or freezer root cellar with limited capability.

You can use the sunken fridge or freezers in places where the temperatures are rather erratic because they are highly insulated. They will keep the internal temperatures fairly constant and stop outside moisture from penetrating.

Instructions

1. Get an old or defective fridge or freezer.

2. Remove the fridge or freezer's complete working component set, including the mechanical components, by removing its backside. You will just be left with the fridge's shell.

3. Once you've got the fridge's shell, you must begin poking holes into the rear. To drill holes, attach a drill bit to your drill. It works just fine but don't worry if the plastic cracks. The holes are essential in every way. This permits air to enter the root cellar from the ground.

During the cold season, your vegetables won't freeze because the air below the ground hovers around 45-degrees which is still okay for your vegetables for this type of root cellar.

4. Cover the openings with a bug net. Although this fridge will be dug underground, you can't be too sure when creepy crawlies will find their way into your root cellar.

5. Drill holes above and beneath the fridge. This is once more a matter of airflow. This enables air to flow up to the surface via the openings at the bottom. Don't sweat; if done properly (enough circulation), this won't let the cold air in.

6. Attach pipes to the fridge's ends. The pipe's length will vary depending on how deep you intend to bury your root cellar into the ground. The pipes protruded approximately 3 feet from the ground in this root cellar. Vents were also installed above the pipes to prevent dirt and water from falling into the pipes and entering the root cellar.

7. If you can, use a backhoe to dig a large hole into the ground to make the process faster; else, do so manually. Again, your fridge's size and how deep you wish the hole to be must be considered. However, it must be at least 3 to 4 feet deep to attain below the freezing level. The fridge can be dug into a good ground spot around your house.

8. Lay a level stack of bricks or rocks beneath the fridge. This makes the airflow better.

9. Put the fridge into the ground, where it will rest permanently. If you are installing it close to a structure, ensure that there is sufficient space to easily access the door. Fill in the dirt

10. Make space that surrounds the fridge. As seen below, there is a little box built around a board positioned next to the fridge. This was done to prevent dirt from being kicked in when the fridge is opened and because it's ideal to have a big, hefty cover sitting above the fridge;

although it is clumsy, it effectively prevents the fridge from becoming really cold.

It was covered with a top for two basic reasons.

- Because of young kids, there's no need to cause an accident.

- It becomes cold in the middle of winter. The top of the fridge was insulated before covering it with a top. This reduces the amount of cold wind that would otherwise cause the fridge's top to become frozen.

11. Put your produce inside the fridge and cover it with a layer of sawdust, straw, or sand. Ensure to

provide them with adequate spacing to allow airflow between the produce. If you'd like, you can put your multiple small items (such as apples, etc.) in burlap sacks and put them in the sunken fridge.

Things to note

- Install a temperature-sensitive plug inside the fridge that will trigger a light bulb to be turned on when the temperature attains the freezing point, potentially preventing your produce from spoiling. Your fridge can be kept from freezing with a simple halogen light bulb, and when the temperature rises beyond the freezing point, it will switch off.

- This refrigerator-based root cellar alternative might also struggle to maintain a temperature below 45° during summer. It's recommended to remove the majority of your vegetables by May.

Bucket Root Cellar

Before wrapping things up, let's look at another low-budget, non-traditional root cellar alternative. As you are aware, plastic has a very long lifespan. Additionally, it is not significantly impacted by changes in temperature and does not rust compared to steel. Hence, plastic is recommended when using the bucket root cellar alternative. Again, this type of root cellar comes with limited capabilities.

Materials needed include;

- Drill

- Large drill bit

- Shovel, and

- 5-gallon plastic bucket(s) with lids

You have the option of using buckets you currently own or purchasing new ones. Before starting any activity, wash and dry the buckets if they have been used.

Instructions

1. Turn the bucket upside down to make several holes in its bottom. Your produce wouldn't have mushy bottoms because these holes enable the produce within the bucket

to keep a uniform temperature and provide an escape route for moisture to exit the bottom of the bucket into the soil. Drill a single hole at the center, working your way out by drilling four or five uniformly spaced holes around the middle, and finally, five to six holes scattered toward the outside of the bucket's bottom.

2. Pick a spot for your Root Cellar. The produce won't be as influenced by changes in temperature if you pick a spot close to your home. The spot you pick should also provide protection from certain elements and bad weather.

3. Make a hole in your designated spot. The hole must be slightly broader than your bucket's

size and around 2 ft deep. When you have finished digging, backfill the hole until the bucket is firmly planted into the hole, and press the soil down the sides of the bucket.

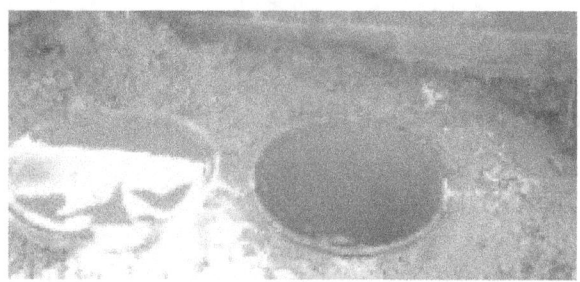

4. Choose your favorite root vegetables to stock the bucket with; carrots, onions, or potatoes preserve well in this kind of environment. Carrots have green tops that should be removed, leaving just a tiny stub of green at the top. Your carrots, potatoes, and onions can be brushed clean from dirt if you'd like, but don't wash them!

Note

To prevent your produce from rotting in storage, you should spread them apart and cover them with sand, straw, or sawdust, which are perfect for maintaining uniform humidity.

What Not to Store in a Root Cellar Alternative

Right now, traditional root cellars are ideal for keeping practically anything. Despite having the word "root" in its name, people preserve virtually most food in it, from ceramic sauerkraut crocks to home-canned jams.

These inexpensive alternatives can't store nearly the same foods and are not quite as flexible. A traditional root cellar has much more room and sturdy shelves to hold jars, cans, crocks, and others.

Root cellar alternatives can become very colder than traditional ones, particularly if you use materials that are not properly insulated.

Due to this reason, glass jars holding pickles, soup, or preserves may break. In addition to wasting great food, this erases lots of hard work and contaminates the rest of the container.

Therefore, only preserve root vegetables and produce with thick skin, and you will be fine.

A Short message from the Author:

Hey, I hope you are enjoying the book? I would love to hear your thoughts!

Many readers do not know how hard reviews are to come by and how much they help an author.

I would be incredibly grateful if you could take just 60 seconds to write a short review on Amazon, even if it is a few sentences!

>> Click here to leave a quick review

Thanks for the time taken to share your thoughts!

Chapter 4

Root Cellar Mistakes To Avoid

Even though constructing a root cellar is a big task, it is well worth the cost if you want to live off the grid, be prepared for an emergency, or want to revert to the age-long traditional way of preserving foods.

Nevertheless, several mistakes must be avoided entirely when planning and constructing a root cellar; some or all have been previously discussed but require more attention.

Insufficient ventilation

A root cellar has to maintain the correct temperature, humidity, and ventilation levels to let clean air in and foul air out. The ethylene gas produced by some vegetables and fruits is one of the grounds behind the requirement for air exchange. Other foods will decay faster if a large amount of this gas is present.

Food will dry out if the humidity is very low, causing mildew, mold, and rot in the process if the humidity is very high. Vents should be installed high up to expel stale air and gas and also installed close to the ground to introduce clean air.

When ventilation is being installed, ensure that you choose vents that allow you to control the airflow and enclose the opening of the vents with a screen to prevent critters from entering.

Vegetables and fruits being kept so close to each other

In the previous part, I addressed ethylene gas, a gas that some vegetables and fruits generate that can harm other vegetables and fruits. These food should thus be kept apart.

In the earlier part of chapter 2, I made a long list of foods that produces ethylene gas and foods that are bound to rot if placed close to them; so kindly refer to that section of this book. Also, if the foods you want to store in your root cellar were not captured in the list, investigate the foods you intend to store before you stock your root cellar.

Additionally, you must design your root cellar with the production of ethylene gas in consideration while setting up the shelves and storage sections.

Not having enough darkness

Most of the foods you wish to store in your root cellar are sworn enemies of light. Potatoes, for instance, might sprout when exposed to light, while other vegetables and fruits can lose their color and nutrition as a result.

You must close any windows in your root cellar if you want to prevent light from entering.

Burlap can be used as an alternative solution to conceal the produce to reduce the impact of light that may enter the root cellar. Again, you can refer to the **root cellar construction requirements** section in chapter 3 for more tips on this.

Not tracking the temperature and humidity levels

There is no justification for not providing an effective technique to regulate and sustain your root cellar's temperature and humidity levels.

Temperature and humidity can be monitored by a vast array of instruments, most of which are inexpensive. You may find a lot of instruments that can provide you with this data and monitor temperature and humidity changes over time. Some instruments can also deliver this information to your smart cellphone.

The ventilation can be adjusted to be more efficient as you keep an eye on the circumstances within your root cellar to get the best possible outcomes.

The truth is you cannot adequately secure your produce if there is no instrument to tell you the temperature and humidity levels.

Making use of concrete floors

Concrete floors have the drawback of preventing moisture from the dirt underneath it from entering the root cellar. Additionally, concrete has a bad propensity to trap heat, which is not good for a root cellar.

Plain dirt is usually a preferable choice when building a root cellar newly and deciding the material to use for the floor. A dirt floor retains cool air while also allowing moisture to enter the root cellar from the ground. Getting the sledgehammer out to rebuild your root cellar's floor is unnecessary if it has already been constructed with a concrete floor. The essential modifications to have a completely operational root cellar can be made, provided you are conscious of the conditions inside your root cellar. Again, you can refer to the root cellar construction requirements section in chapter 3 for more tips on this.

Coming and Going Too Frequently

Root cellars operate better when the essential cool, humid air is kept inside. To ensure your root cellar sustains optimum conditions within it, the door of your cellar should be shut as frequently as possible. Hot air is allowed in and cool air out each time the door is opened, not excluding the heat emitted from your body that also heats up the air within. If you can, avoid storing anything you require frequent access to in your root cellar to lessen the urge to regularly enter the cellar.

Your root cellar is exclusively for storing food, so the one time you should open the door is to add or remove food. Prepare ahead of time by taking sufficient food that will last for several days to avoid going inside the root cellar regularly to get some food.

The end… almost!

Hey! We've made it to the final chapter of this book, and I hope you've enjoyed it so far.

If you have not done so yet, I would be incredibly thankful if you could take just a minute to leave a quick review on Amazon

Reviews are not easy to come by, and as an independent author with a little marketing budget, I rely on you, my readers, to leave a short review on Amazon.

Even if it is just a sentence or two!

Customer Reviews

⭐⭐⭐⭐⭐ 2
5.0 out of 5 stars ▾

5 star		100%
4 star		0%
3 star		0%
2 star		0%
1 star		0%

Share your thoughts with other customers

Write a customer review

See all verified purchase reviews ›

So if you really enjoyed this ook, please...

>> Click here to leave a brief review on Amazon.

I truly appreciate your effort to leave your review, as it truly makes a huge difference.

Chapter 5

Root Cellar FAQs

Below are some frequently asked root cellar questions you can leverage as you consider building your root cellar. Most of what you need to know about root cellar construction has been discussed in detail in the previous chapters.

How long do vegetables stay fresh in a root cellar?

Several foods stay longer in a root cellar's cool, humid climate than they would in other types of storage. Depending on the vegetables stored, they can stay long, from 2-9 months, lasting between 4-6 months on average.

Which direction does a root cellar have to face?

A properly-drained area about 10-20 yards from your home, tucked into a pre-existing soil bank, is the ideal place for a root cellar. To deflect the sun's heat, the door of the root cellar should typically face north.

Can milk and cheese be stored in a root cellar?

Dairy items like milk and cheese can be stored in a root cellar. Milk, when stored, can remain fresh for a maximum of two weeks and cheese for a maximum of six months. Hard cheeses perform better for a prolonged life span than soft cheeses.

Can meat be stored in a root cellar?

Preserved meats stores quite well in a root cellar. Meat products like jerky, salted or smoked pork, pemmican, and other meats that are alike can be stored without problems for several weeks or months. In order to effectively prolong their storage life, fresh meats can as well be stored in a root cellar, such as ham, sausage, bacon, and beef.

Can you store keep eggs in a root cellar?

Yes. Eggs may last for a year when stored in a root cellar that meets the temperature and humidity conditions.

Is a root cellar equivalent to a cold room?

In contrast to a root cellar, a cold room is a completed area in a dry basement that's warm. The design is the primary distinction between a cold room in a basement and a root cellar. You might be able to construct a functional cold room if your basement is partially underground.

Is it possible for seeds to be stored in a root cellar?

Yes. Use materials like plastic jars or glass to ensure that your seeds are shielded from moisture. Alternatively, you can add the silica sacks that are included in shoe boxes to your seed jars to control moisture.

Conclusion

Any homesteader who wants to increase their food independence and security level and preserve their own food throughout the year needs a root cellar.

A root cellar makes a great backup for the conventional refrigeration everyone currently enjoys. You'd have the knowledge and abilities to sustain the security of your food in a grid-down, off-grid, or emergency scenario if you construct a root cellar and use it frequently. It will take time and effort to construct a good root cellar. However, once it is constructed, it will benefit you greatly by keeping your produce fresh for a long time. Time must also be taken to learn from others' mistakes to build and operate a root cellar that meets not only your food consumption needs but one that also ensures the security of your food should a major calamity or the loss of power supply occur.

Let this guidebook be as much as a compass for you as you plan to build your root cellar, regularly referencing any section discussed herein if you are unsure of how to proceed or stuck in-between. I also presume that you have some background knowledge in basic woodworking to help make it a little easier for you to implement.

When you are done with your construction, take a moment to reflect on your progress and celebrate your wins once your root cellar is set up and fully functional; then, take a huge bite out of one of your stored produce, either cultivated or purchased at a local farmer's market – you deserve it.

I wish you all the best!